WHY IS SHE SMILING

Unexpected Joy Discovered by
a Most Unlikely Submissive Wife

Amy Williams

A big thank you goes to my husband, Brett. Your love is strong, true, and a gift I never want to take for granted. Also, I thank my mother, Gail. Your unwavering belief that I can do anything seeped into my heart and bones at an early age. You continue to show me what unconditional love looks like. Most importantly, this book would not exist without God's prompting and guidance. Lord, I am forever grateful for your mercy, grace and for giving me a life so abundant.

CONTENTS

ACKNOWLEDGMENTS

You'll notice I quote my pastor a few times in the book. His name is Dr. Alex Himaya, and he is senior pastor of theChurch.at in Broken Arrow, Ok. If you're interested in hearing powerful, anointed sermons, he's your guy. Visit in person or watch live online at thechurch.at/live

Cover design courtesy of Lesley Zellers. See more of her mad skills at recipeforcrazy.com

Chapter 1
I GET IT

If you'd read the title of this book to me ten years ago, I would've rolled my eyes. Fifteen years ago, I would've laughed at – possibly even pitied – the woman who wrote it. So I get it. Submission sounds antiquated. It's not in style. More often than not, it's mocked. So why on earth did I choose to write about it?

I didn't.

I've always been a writer. Mainly television and radio spots, print ads, websites, etc. But until the winter of 2012, I'd never been inspired to write a book. Then one afternoon, I was on my hands and knees cleaning a toilet. (I'm sure that's how it was for Hemingway.) But right there, in all my rubber-gloved glory, it happened. Thoughts, experiences, and words flooded by brain. I had to type them out immediately.

After five hours of writing, barely stopping long enough to grab a drink, I sat back and realized what had happened. Why now. Why this topic. Why me.

God has something to say. He usually does if we listen. And He doesn't really care what's popular. He cares about us. He knows healing begins with Him, and sustaining joy is found in surrendering to Him, loving Him, and following His instruction. I will tell you from years of experience, it's true.

So, why are you holding this book? Likely because something here hits home...

Your marriage has suffered so much, for so long, you can actually hear the timer beginning to buzz.

You've spent so many years butting heads with your husband, you can't imagine releasing your grip on the anger and frustration in your heart. But you're exhausted and something has to give.

You're newly married, wondering why it's so difficult when you expected it to be so fun.

You're in a decent marriage, but sense there is a higher plane of harmony, and you want to experience it.

Take comfort knowing many other women – down your street and half a world away – feel the same. The search for that elusive harbor of marital joy is a common journey.

I'm glad you're here. So is God. Because this book is really about you, your husband and Him. If you easily bristle at the word "submit," I urge you to stop and pray before reading any further. For real change, God needs fertile soil.

The seed that fell among the thorns represents others who hear God's word, but all too quickly the message is crowded out by the worries of this life, the lure of wealth, and the desire for other things, so no fruit is produced. And the seed that fell on good soil represents those who hear and accept God's word and produce a harvest of thirty, sixty, or even a hundred times as much as had been planted!" Mark 4:18-20

Note: If you're in a physically abusive marriage, you need to protect yourself, your children, and find safety. It is not God's desire that you live in fear of your husband. Seek Christian counsel, asking God to lead your steps and give you wisdom as to how to move forward.

If any of you lacks wisdom, let him ask God, who gives generously to all without reproach, and it will be given him.

James 1:5

****

For the first 32 years of my life, I had no plans of being subject to a man. Just the thought of marriage was a stretch. I had a successful career, and no trouble finding a new relationship to replace the last. Growing up, I had a front row seat for what marriage had to offer. I witnessed verbal and physical abuse, indifference and infidelity. My mother and grandmothers had three failed marriages each. If you're counting, that's nine marriages in the gutter.

I remember telling people as a little girl if I ever did marry, I was waiting until I was at least thirty. I would take my time and find a guy I could actually stand to be with forever. And by forever, I meant something like ten years.

I made certain I didn't need a man to take care of me financially. I'd spent too many childhood nights watching my mom curled up in the corner of our couch with a pen, paper, and calculator trying to figure out how we'd pay the electric bill. There was no man around to do it then, why would I think there ever would be?

I accepted Jesus as my savior when I was young, and vaguely knew there were scriptures directed at husbands and wives. But was anyone really paying attention to them? Over the years I saw only a handful of inspiring Christian marriages. The rarity kind of bummed me out.

Despite all this, once I met my husband, the fairytale visions bubbled to the surface. I loved him. He loved me. Could we be the exception? Could we make it to that practically unheard of happy ending? I was in big-time love. He bought a beautiful ring and proposed with such hope in his eyes.

I had to try.

About three months into our engagement we began attending church. The kind where it felt like revival every Sunday. We made that little church our home the first few years of marriage, and I'll always be grateful for it. The preaching was honest and intense. I remember after the first visit, my fiancé was unsettled by the thought of going again. He later told me he knew if we went back he'd have to fully surrender to God. He was right. The next week, he practically jumped over the pew during the alter call. He was sweating with tears in his eyes. After praying with the pastor, he came back to me visibly shaken. He'd given everything to God, and there was no going back. Without that decision, I don't know if he and I would share the same address today.

During our premarital counseling, the pastor told us, "*You have to take divorce off the table.*" He wasn't kidding, not even a little. My fiancé – without hesitating – nodded in full agreement. I, however, was reeling. *Could I actually do that?* I thought divorce kind of went with marriage. Like batteries come with a new toy. When the toy dies, use these. When the marriage dies, use this.

There in the pastor's office, I shook off the fear, put on my big girl panties and agreed – divorce was off the table. If I was going to pledge forever to one man in front of my family, friends, and most importantly God, I was going to mean it. But what would that kind of marriage look like? Once it went bad – and didn't it always? I'd just suck it up, stay and keep my promise.

But hallelujah that was never what God intended. He created marriage to be a blessing, not a curse. And as the creator of marriage, He knows how it works best. He gives us detailed, almost shockingly simple instructions. And once I followed them – with my whole heart – everything changed.

Submit to one another out of reverence for Christ. Wives, be subject to your own husbands, as to the Lord. For the husband is the head of the wife, as Christ also is the head of the church, He Himself being the Savior of the body. But as the church is subject to Christ, so also the wives ought to be to their husbands in everything. Husbands, love your wives, just as Christ also loved the church and gave Himself up for her; that He might sanctify her, having cleansed her by the washing of water with the word, that He might present to Himself the church in all her glory, having no spot or wrinkle or any such thing; but that she should be holy and blameless. So husbands ought also to love their own wives as their own bodies. He who loves his own wife loves himself; for no one ever hated his own flesh, but nourishes and cherishes it, just as Christ also does the church, because we are members of His body. For this cause a man shall leave his father and mother and shall cleave to his wife; and the two shall become one flesh. This mystery is great; but I am speaking with reference to Christ and the church. Nevertheless let each individual among you also love his own wife even as himself; and let the wife see to it that she respects her husband.

Ephesians 5:21-33

Chapter 2
THE FIRST TEST

The first test popped up sooner than I hoped. I felt the prompting in my heart.

The money.

Lord, what do you mean, the money? Oh. The money.

The three thousand dollars I had sitting in a bank account from my single days. The money I subconsciously thought of as my safety net. The money I'd "forgotten" to tell my husband about. God brought it before my eyes, causing me to look at it for what it really was – my anticipation of a failed marriage.

I tried to push it out of my mind. But I was completely unsettled. I could feel God waiting for me to obey.

You could argue – which I tried – "*Lord, it's not like he asked me about it and I lied to him.*" I soon learned this decision, like so many in marriage, isn't just about me and my husband. It's about me and God.

So whoever knows the right thing to do and fails to do it, for him it is sin. James 4:17

The rubber was meeting the road. Did I truly trust God? Would I be obedient to Him, or put my trust in the three thousand dollars? I came home from work that day, sat my husband down on the couch, and told him about it through teary eyes. His confusion broke my heart. He didn't understand why it made me so anxious to cut down my safety net. He was so sure of us.

What happened soon after surprised me. My husband and God became my safety net. I was more emotionally invested in my marriage, and I was trusting God like never before. I felt free. Like a little girl who sleeps soundly at night, I had people who loved me looking out for me. A husband and Father who would lay down their life for me. That security made three thousand dollars look like chump change.

Chapter 3
THE HEART

Yes, I am the vine; you are the branches. Those who remain in me, and I in them, will produce much fruit. For apart from me you can do nothing. John 15:5

So, how do we go about the heart change required to willingly be subject to a man, who – like us – was born a sinner? Who like us will undoubtedly stumble, fail, and disappoint? First we need to fully submit to God. Relying on him for everything. Resting in the vine. Because the only way we can live out God's command is to have Jesus living in us and through us.

Being subject to, and respecting our husbands, will be a natural outflow of our relationship with God. We simply cannot achieve one without the other. If you're already starting to sweat at the idea of letting your husband lead, back up and make sure you've given your life to God. If you're unsure, that's where you begin. At the end of this book you'll find the exact scriptures needed to begin your relationship with God. It's the wisest decision you'll ever make.

Once you have that settled, buckle up. Because obeying God's command of submitting to your husband means breaking away from the world's lies. It takes guts, determination and work. It takes God.

Put on then, as God's chosen ones, holy and beloved, compassionate hearts, kindness, humility, meekness, and patience, bearing with one another and, if one has a complaint against another, forgiving each other; as the Lord has forgiven you, so you also must forgive. And above all these put on love, which binds everything together in perfect harmony. Colossians 3:12-14

We know God isn't interested in a tithe given with a begrudging heart. He's also not interested in submission with a defiant heart. Sure, we can let our husband have final say on a decision, but if we leave the room in a huff after shooting him a *"you'll regret this"* look, there's zero love in our actions. There's no humility to our obedience.

Come near to God and he will come near to you. Wash your hands, you sinners, and purify your hearts, you double-minded. James 4:8

We can't be double minded in our decision to submit. There's no joy to be experienced when we resolve, *"I'll do it, but I'm not going to like it."* Because it's very possible to go through the submissive motions, and your heart still be far from God. As the scripture above says, when we're double minded, we must draw near to God, wash our hands of sin and purify our hearts. Only then can we be wholly committed to being the wife He's calling us to be.

Authentic submission flows out of a heart of humility. Too often, people confuse humility with humiliate. Completely different. Humility isn't something awful done to you, it's a respectful, gentle heart attitude you purposefully embrace. C.S. Lewis said it this way, *"True humility is not thinking less of yourself, it's thinking of yourself less."*

9

It's more than a gift to your husband; it's a gift to everyone around you. When I think of the people I most enjoy, the ones who truly bless my heart, they're the ones who practice humility.

When you catch yourself being double-minded or inauthentic in your submission, get alone with God and ask him for a heart of humility.

The fear of the Lord is instruction in wisdom, and humility comes before honor. Proverbs 15:33

Do nothing from selfish ambition or conceit, but in humility count others more significant than yourselves. Philippians 2:3

Chapter 4
DROPPING THE "IF"

With my whole heart I seek you; let me not wander from your commandments! I have stored up your word in my heart, that I might not sin against you. Psalm 119: 10-11

There's a good chance you're already thinking – in a whisper or defiant shout – *"But my husband doesn't deserve my respect and submission."*

Thankfully, we don't have to wait for our husbands to be perfect before we can be obedient to God. But a genuine breakthrough in our attitude, behavior, and marriage does require grabbing hold of this truth.

> **Biblical submission and respect**
> **is not a reaction to, or dependent**
> **on our husband's behavior.**
> **It is individual obedience**
> **to our Father's command.**

More simply, it's not about your husband deserving it. It's about God deserving it.

And do not be fooled. When we as Christian women choose to ignore the scripture, we are openly, willfully, rebelling. We're sinning. We're telling God we know better than He. We cannot tear pages from the bible, and we cannot expect our marriage to be blessed without following the instruction of the One who created it.

Many women read, *"be subject"* and *"respect,"* but in their head actually hear, *"be subject and respect **if**..."*

Your husband is smarter than you.
He makes more money than you.
His faith is stronger than yours.
He treats you like a queen.
He does more right than wrong.

But there is no "if." God didn't include a list of qualifications our husbands must meet before we submit and respect. They meet the criteria simply by being our husband.

We want to argue. We plead with God saying, *"But my husband doesn't love me like you've told him to. He doesn't provide financially like he's supposed to. He doesn't lead as you've called him. I promise Lord, when he starts doing his part, I'll do mine."*

But God simply looks us in the eyes, and lovingly tells us *our* part. As always, His ways are higher than ours. Instead of viewing submission and respect as our husband's reward, we can choose to bring glory to God by submitting to and respecting our husbands despite their behavior. We can do it because we authentically love God and our heart chases after pleasing Him.

If you're harboring unforgiveness in your heart, you can choose to truly forgive. You can stop making him suffer for what he's done in the past. Then – and only then – can you begin being the wife God intended. If you can do that, get excited. When we're not holding on to past hurts, our arms are open to receive blessing. How cool is that?

We begin by embracing His word. We accept that we are not responsible for our husband's obedience. We can lean on Jesus to help us with our own.

Chapter 5
SEEDS OR WEEDS

A wise man's heart guides his mouth, and his lips promote instruction. Pleasant words are a honeycomb, sweet to the soul and healing to the bones. Proverbs 16:23-24

Making a genuine effort to respect our spouse, to build him up instead of tearing him down, requires a realization. Through seemingly harmless words that fall out of our mouth, we are emotionally cutting our husbands deeply.

"Whatever."

"You don't have a clue."

"If you made more money, we wouldn't have this problem."

"You could learn a few things from (so-and-so's) husband."

"It's none of your business."

At the core of all these statements is, *"I don't respect you."*

Ask a husband about past hurts in his marriage, and most all of them can be traced to his wife's disrespect. You might argue it was simply a reaction to his hurtfulness or neglect. You'll notice it did no good.

In both everyday and extreme moments of anger, hurt or frustration, our fleshly instinct is to injure. Our heart races, ready to pounce, to prove our superiority, to savor the taste of our *"take that!"* speech. But the cost is high. And the damage can be lasting.

The acidic words, directed with precision at the one you love, actually drain back down your throat into your heart and flesh. You share in the pain. Why? Because God has made you one flesh.

For this reason a man will leave his father and mother and be united to his wife, and the two will become one flesh. So they are no longer two, but one flesh. Therefore what God has joined together, let no one separate. Mark 10:7-9

During our first year of marriage, my husband and I had several fights – some real doozies. After a while, I realized at the heart of every one of them was a power struggle. We were fighting to be heard, to be right, to win. My flesh cried out in frustration that he was wrong, and therefore I should hold the power. But even after winning a fight, I sensed I was losing something far more important. My husband wouldn't just walk away sorry, he was emotionally defeated. I remember hearing him tell someone that he hated fighting with me because I was "too good at it."

Ouch. The Holy Spirit revealed I was setting fire to our love with my tongue. The kind of fire that's claimed far too many marriages. Since then, I've been incredibly careful with my words and intent. Our disagreements now are pretty rare, and the tone is far more respectful. We've learned to express our feelings without damaging our relationship. I've learned to reign in my words, putting

15

God's instruction before my pride.

Know this, my beloved brothers; let every person be quick to hear, slow to speak, slow to anger; for the anger of man does not produce the righteousness of God. James 1:19-20

And look closely, because disrespect takes many shapes. Beyond demeaning words at home or in front of others, you can disrespect him by being dishonest, financially irresponsible, physically denying him or emotionally punishing him. Or by telling your children through words or actions that ignoring what daddy wants is acceptable – that in fact, *you* have final say.

These actions, little or grand in scale, chip away at the foundation of marriage. Thankfully, we can choose to show respect. When it's the last thing we want to do – when it's the last thing they *expect* us to do – it could be the first thing we need to do. This is our chance to look like Jesus. We can respond with kindness, forgiveness and understanding. This is our opportunity to plant seeds of abundance instead of weeds that choke out love.

So pray for wisdom when it comes to your speech. My pastor once wisely said, *"You're either building a garden or a grave with your words."* So always consider, is what I'm about to say moving our marriage closer to a garden or a grave?

Remember, you cannot hurt your husband without hurting yourself. The good news is the reverse is also true. You cannot bless your husband without blessing yourself. You cannot love him without loving yourself. Commit this to your heart. You and he are one.

An excellent wife who can find? She is far more precious than jewels. The heart of her husband trusts in her, and he will have no lack of gain. She does him good, and not harm, all the days of her life. Proverbs 31:10-12

We wonder why there aren't more strong male leaders in the church today. Yet, so many of us are challenging these men at home, stepping in front of them at every turn, "*Honey, I've got this. I know better. I'll take care of it.*"

If we're a roadblock to our husbands fulfilling their role of leadership in the home, how can we possibly – with any authenticity – encourage them to be leaders in the church and world? If we're telling them through words or actions they aren't smart enough, strong enough, that we don't trust them enough to lead our family, is it any wonder they don't feel confident enough to lead once they step off the front porch?

And it's not just what we say to our husbands, it's what we say about them. See, there's a crazy rumor floating around that women like to gossip. We usually try to mask it as concern, but really we're just airing dirty laundry. While we should strive to not gossip at all, we certainly need to leave our husbands out of the chitchat.

Nothing good comes from filling someone's ear with our husband's faults, habits or failures. We may tell ourselves it's harmless, but in reality we're tearing down their reputation, belittling them, betraying their trust – certainly not acting as their advocate and partner.

We're called to respect our husbands. We should hold them in high esteem, focusing on the good and praying about the bad. In Isaiah, we read one of God's names is Wonderful Counselor. This is great news. We have our very own counselor who created us. He knows our husbands and us inside and out. He and His word are the ultimate source of wisdom. Not our mother. Not our neighbor. And definitely not our self-proclaimed man-hater buddy from college.

Remember, you and your husband are one. When you tarnish his character, publicize his faults and cut him down, you're doing it to yourself. Think back to the look on Rocky Balboa's face when Adrian said, "*You can't win!*" Ugh. Heartbreaking. So lift your husband up. Brag about him. Be his biggest fan, his safe place, the person he knows has his back. Most importantly, be a wife he can trust.

Draw a line in the sand. "*I will no longer be a stumbling block for my husband.*" With God's help, you'll find yourself being supportive, encouraging. You become his partner rather than his opponent. This attitude of obedience unfolds blessings without end, reaching your heart, his, your children, and the watching world.

Chapter 6
GIVING IT TO GOD

Cast your burden on the Lord, and he will sustain you; he will never permit the righteous to be moved. Psalm 55:22

My husband's love of motorcycles was clear when we met. And at first, the whole bad-boy-on-a-Harley thing is pretty enticing. But watching the father of your toddler straddle a hard tail and ride away can make you frantic with worry.

I made no bones about it – I did not like him riding. I didn't think the thrill was worth the risk. But I also didn't ask or tell him to sell his motorcycle. After a year or so, he decided to sell it so we could pay off some debt. Yea! I was so relieved, but knew deep down it wasn't the last motorcycle that would occupy our garage.

I was right. Less than two years later, along came a deal too good for him to pass up. He clearly had the itch. I'd watch him silently stare at bikers on the open road, knowing he longed to join them. Funny thing, when you truly love someone, you find yourself willing to do anything to make them happy. Including agreeing to another motorcycle.

This time when he bought the bike, I didn't give him the speech. Why should I? He knew my opinion hadn't changed. Drowning him with guilt would only suck all the fun out of his new toy. A wise wife never wants to be resented, or to diminish her husband's joy.

So I prayed.

God knew my heart and my concerns. He also knew I was being obedient by turning it over to Him. About eight months went by. And honestly, the bike just became part of our world. My husband wore his helmet if he went outside town limits or on the highway. It was actually saving us gas money. I'd learned to deal.

One day he casually mentioned that his father suggested he sell the motorcycle. *What?* When my husband was growing up, his father allowed him to do crazy dangerous stunts on everything from a 4-wheeler to a jet ski without so much as raising an eyebrow. But now, he persisted.

Every few days, his father would mention the bike was too dangerous, or share a story of someone who'd been in a horrible accident. Even my husband's boss began chiming in with agreement. While I appreciated their concern, I knew if my husband really wanted to keep the motorcycle, it was staying.

About a month later, it was my birthday weekend. My husband said he had a surprise for me. It wasn't ready, but he was so excited he couldn't wait. *"I'm buying you a 1972, cherry red, fully restored Chevy truck – the one you've always wanted."*

I was speechless. Extremely excited, but even more confused. I mean, where would we get the money? He understood the puzzled look on my face.

"I'm selling my bike to pay for it."

WHAT?

You'd think elation or relief would've been my first reaction. It wasn't.

"*No,*" I blurted out. "*No, no, no. You're not going to sell your bike and resent me for it.*"

"*Babe, I want this. I've been praying about it, and I really feel like it's the right thing to do. For us and our family. We can enjoy this truck together. And dad's right, I have a family to think about. I'm not saying I'll never own another motorcycle, but right now, this is what I want to do.*"

I could barely process the information. Not only was he selling the bike, he was doing it to make a dream of mine come true. Oh God in heaven, you are faithful and good.

Now to him who is able to do far more abundantly than all that we ask or think, according to the power at work within us, to him be the glory in the church and in Christ Jesus throughout all generations, forever and ever. Amen. Ephesians 3:20-22

What if I'd chosen to throw a fit at the first mention of buying the motorcycle? What if I'd berated him every time he went for a ride? How would this story have ended? I would've represented chains instead of freedom, anger instead of trust. There would've been no blessing to be gained.

Chapter 7
SEARCH MY HEART

It is better to live in a desert land than with a quarrelsome and nagging wife. Proverbs 21:19

I've never liked the word "nag." Probably because of the image it conjures up – a cranky woman in a faded pink housecoat, hair in curlers, wagging her finger, harping about the same thing over and over. And while there are always things to be done and issues to address, you have a choice. Rather than repeatedly begging your husband to do something, you can give it over to God. In plain words, tell God you trust him to work on your husband's heart in this area.

Then really, truly give it to God. Lay it at his feet and do not rush back to pick it up in five minutes, five hours or five days. Try expecting the best, instead of the worst. Let your husband surprise you. Let him come through for you. Trust God to reward your obedience, like a father does a child. Because He is your Father.

You parents – if your children ask for a loaf of bread, do you give them a stone instead? Or if they ask for a fish, do you give them a snake? Of course not! So if you sinful people know how to give good gifts to your children, how much more will your heavenly Father give good gifts to those who ask him. Matthew 7:9-11

I've tried this with everything from washing dishes to major financial decisions. And in those instances where I truly give it to God, one of two things happens. Either my husband eventually comes through for me exactly as I hoped, or God changes my attitude instead of changing my circumstances. He does a work in my heart. He lovingly adjusts my expectations and lines up my desires with His will.

Delight yourself in the Lord and he will give you the desires of your heart. Psalm 37:4

****

Seems all my life I've been asking God to reveal His plans. *Where should I go to college, which career should I choose, who will my husband be, would I look good in a pixie cut...*

I remember my pastor saying something that opened my eyes and hit me square in the heart: *How can we expect God to provide specific instruction, when we don't follow His general instruction?*

We want all the answers, but too often we ignore instruction He's already given. *"But,"* you say, *"I know the ten commandments. I don't lie, cheat, steal, murder..."* And that's great. But just as we can't pick and choose which commandments we like, we can't ignore what God asks us to do in our marriage. Submitting is more than our responsibility to our husband; it's part of our complete obedience to God.

Listen! The Lord's arm is not too weak to save you, nor is his ear too deaf to hear you call. It's your sins that have cut you off from God. Because of your sins, he has turned away and will not listen anymore. Isaiah 59:1-2

Next time you're praying, ask Him to search your heart. Ask Him to reveal any general instructions you're not following. It could be forgiveness you're withholding, gossip you've been spreading, or maybe you're not showing your husband respect. Whatever it is, address it with the sincerity of David.

Search me, God, and know my heart; test me and know my anxious thoughts. See if there is any offensive way in me, and lead me in the way everlasting. Psalm 139:23-24

For the record, I would not look good in a pixie cut.

Chapter 8
THE HELPER

The Lord God said, 'It is not good for the man to be alone. I will make a helper suitable for him. Genesis 2:18

Confession time. When I originally read Genesis 2:18, I felt a bit insulted. Okay, maybe more than a bit. I mean, a *helper?* But God, I have so much more to offer. After all, I'd been successfully taking care of myself for over a decade. Now I'm supposed to step aside and wait for my husband to need me?

Helper. What does that even look like?

I painted this crazy mental picture of my husband as a surgeon (which he's not) performing some amazing lifesaving transplant. There I stood, quietly in the shadows until he says, "*Scalpel.*" And I place it in his hand. That's it. That's all. I'm the helper.

Thankfully, God has revealed the truth of this scripture and I've been able to shake that ridiculous vision. See, when God looked at Adam, he realized there were talents, gifts and abilities he lacked. That's why He created Eve. She was different. She brought something new to the table. If Adam had been sufficient and just needed an extra set of hands, God would've just made another Adam. Praise Jesus, our role is so much more than simply handing over the scalpel.

And let's not forget, when we're called a helper, we're in excellent company.

But when the Helper comes, whom I will send to you from the Father, the Spirit of truth, who proceeds from the Father, he will bear witness about me. John 15:26

If the Holy Spirit is called the helper, it's time I check my ego at the door and embrace this role as the blessing God intended it to be. Once you do the same, there is no limit to the transforming power you'll experience in your marriage.

****

Serving the demands of our own selfish desires is easy. That's what children do. But it takes maturity and self-discipline to be subject to another human. Our enemy – Satan – tells us our husbands don't deserve our respect. But remember, the enemy has a goal.

The thief comes only to steal, kill and destroy. I came that they may have life and have it abundantly. John 10:10

Abundant life includes a blessed marriage. God wants that for us, so He doesn't leave us in the dark as to how we can experience it. He gives men and women equally important instruction. Wives are to submit and respect. Husbands are to love us as Christ loves the church. But if our husband is the head, what does that make us? Lowly? A servant? And if so, why does that leave such a bad taste in our mouth? Because the world tells us a servant has less worth. But Jesus shows us it is the highest form of love.

For the Son of Man came not to be served but to serve others and to give his life as a ransom for many. Matthew 20:28

Let each of you look not only to his own interests, but also to the interests of others. Have this mind among yourselves, which is yours in Christ Jesus, who though he was in the form of God, did not count equality with God a thing to be grasped, but emptied himself, by taking the form of a servant, being born in the likeness of men. And being found in human form, he humbled himself by becoming obedient to the point of death, even death on a cross. Philippians 2:4-8

See, we're not less than our husband; rather God has made our roles beautifully different. When a storybook character has two heads, it's a monster. That's a pretty good marriage illustration. God made our husbands to be the head, yet we wrestle to share that same space. It's a power struggle that's exhausting and gets ugly pretty quick. Thankfully, there's an alternative. Embracing our role, instead of fighting for one we were never intended to hold, releases us to a joy and freedom the world will never recognize.

When we're free from the responsibilities we were never intended to have, we're free to flourish in the role we were designed to fulfill. We have more energy. We have more time to thoughtfully parent, create a peaceful home, and contribute to our community.

I've discovered when I accept that the whole kit and kaboodle isn't resting on my shoulders, I'm not as spent at the end of the day, which can result in more energy for intimacy. See, God designed marriage to work fluidly, to be a blessing. When we twist it and try to redefine our roles, we distort its natural beauty. We make it a noose around our neck rather than jewels.

By submitting, you're simply acknowledging he has final say. Some of you just spewed Diet Coke across the room. Final say? That sounds like a dictatorship. Unless your husband is abusing his blessing of being head of household, it won't be a dictatorship. Dictators don't love their subjects, they love power. Husbands are commanded to love us – even to the point of death.

There's actually a cool byproduct of him having final say. One I've witnessed in my home and others where wives allow their husband to lead. When our husbands truly sense they're in the driver's seat, when we're not yelling directions in their ear – they make better decisions. Why? I believe there's something about watching us put our trust in their hand that brings out their protective nature, they want to do what's best for us.

But don't kick your feet up for a siesta too quickly. Letting our spouse lead doesn't absolve us of all responsibility. Actually, it just absolves us of one – being in command of our husbands. Off the top of my head, I'm the primary caregiver and life teacher of our son, which is definitely no small matter. I'm shaping a human. I'm responsible for what our family eats, wears, the doctors we see, the media our child digests, oh, and our finances.

Wait a second, finances? Some would say whoever controls the wallet, controls the marriage. Not so. In my family, I monitor spending, pay bills and manage our savings. We both agreed to this arrangement. If he had chosen to take care of our finances, I would've let him. If in the future he chooses to take control of them, he will do so without resistance from me.

Now don't be misled, being submissive and respectful doesn't mean I'm sitting in a quaint wooden chair in the corner waiting for him to allow me to speak. C'mon. We're partners. He values my opinion. He not only listens to it, he asks for it and takes it into account when making family decisions.

And no, we don't agree on everything. To name a few, we don't like the same music, cheer for the same football team, or see eye-to-eye on driving. What he calls skilled road maneuvering, I call aggressive. So like anyone else, we've had some pretty weighty, heated arguments. But I learned early on, one way to quit locking horns is to lose my horns. If my winning a fight causes our marriage to suffer, then we both lose.

For years now, when my husband and I are facing a major decision, the flow typically goes like this. We talk through the pros, cons, our hopes and concerns. We pray and give God time to talk to us. Then I tell him what I feel we should do, followed by something along the lines of, *"But I trust you. Whatever decision you make, I'll support."*

Are you sweating yet? If so, I understand. There's always the chance he'll make a poor decision. But while the situation may not go like you hope, your marriage is still in tact, probably even stronger because you put your trust in him. You didn't just tell him you respect him, you showed him.

Chapter 9
TOSSING THE SCORECARD

Love is patient and kind. Love is not jealous or boastful or proud or rude. It does not demand its own way. It is not irritable, and it keeps no record of being wronged. 1 Corinthians 13:4-5

When you live out God's design for marriage, your relationship will look different. It may not be instant, but it will penetrate every crevice of your life.

You actually stop keeping score.

Hard to believe, I know. In every relationship before this, I was a world-class scorekeeper. My mental file cabinet of past wrongs was full, organized, and at the ready. But I'm here to tell you, when you decide to be *for* your husband, you stop leaping at every opportunity to combat him. You stop filing away all the wrongs to be used as weapons in future duals. And haven't we already been told to do that?

Forgiving fully is so refreshing. It frees us to let go and trust for better going forward. At first it may feel so foreign you question your sanity. *Am I crazy for being kind when my flesh is crying out to retaliate? Am I putting myself in a vulnerable position by letting my husband lead?* The truth is, you are going against everything the world and the devil would tell you. You are being vulnerable to the will of God. But know this, it is much more profitable to be pliable to God's will than to be immovable in your own.

Like God's word, your efforts will not return void. But here's the key. Don't expect a fair transaction. Just as every husband is different, so is every reaction. He may respond with anything from a silent nod of thanks, to sweeping you off your feet and kissing you like a sailor returning from months at sea.

Somewhere along the way, we bought the lie that we should expect a lot, yet do little. Talk about backward. Ask your grandma or grandpa – or anyone north of 60 years old. They were taught the exact opposite. Expect little, do a lot.

We'd do well to soak up the time-tested wisdom of our elders. Don't put your deeds on one side of the scale and your husband's on the other. In fact, toss out the scale. Take a sledgehammer to it. Because it's not about being even. It's about giving more than you ever expect in return.

That's exactly how God loves us, and how He's called us to love each other. It's also the key to avoiding a life of disappointment. It's not easy, but I can tell you from experience, you will find overflowing freedom and relief by simply tearing up the scorecard.

Remember, the Lord will water even the tiniest seed. You simply make a daily choice to be faithful, patiently waiting to see the beauty break forth. And let us not be naive. This battle is bigger than our marriage. With each decision, we are giving ground to God or to the devil.

For we are not fighting against flesh-and-blood enemies, but against evil rulers and authorities of the unseen world, against mighty powers in this dark world, and against evil spirits in the heavenly places. Ephesians 6:12

And now, dear brothers and sisters, one final thing. Fix your thoughts on what is true, and honorable, and right, and pure, and lovely, and admirable. Think about things that are excellent and worthy of praise. Philippians 4:8

One of my worst habits – one I had to actively pray about – is having arguments with my husband entirely in my head. Have you done this? It's draining and a total waste of time. Turns out, after talking about it with my friends, it's pretty common among women. I don't know why I do it, because I always feel the physical ramifications. That stress line from my shoulder blade to the top of my neck seizes up. I get headaches. I don't sleep as well. I'm pretty sure it's responsible for some of my wrinkles.

It goes something like this. He comes in after mowing the lawn, and the Holy Spirit prompts me to thank my husband. *What?* (I recoil in my head) *It's not like he thanks me for making dinner or doing the dishes. Why should I thank him? In fact, he only has to mow about half the year, whereas I have to cook and clean daily...*

And that's all it takes. I'm officially ticked off. And what's he done? Oh right, he mowed the lawn. What a jerk! Ha. Big HA.

So I've prayed about it, asking God to soften my heart and remove any residue of bitterness. He did exactly that. Over time, I learned to stop the destructive inner dialogue. I've learned to show appreciation, to say thank you for things like mowing the lawn. The first time I did, a few days later, when I wasn't expecting it, he came up behind me and wrapped his arms around my waist. *"Thanks for everything you do babe. I mean it."*

We're so much more likely to get the response we desire when we step out in faith and show moment-by-moment obedience to even the smallest prompting from God.

Fixing your eyes on Jesus and setting your mind to obeying God's command isn't a one-time decision. You must choose it every morning. Letting your husband lead means denying your fleshly instincts. At first, it will seem foreign, completely counter intuitive. It's actually just counter world. It goes against the propaganda we're fed nonstop from media.

Television, music and movies tell us to look out for ourselves first. If our husband comes up short? Retaliate. Spend. Cheat. Leave. But those are the weak ways of the world. God calls us to bear fruits of the spirit.

But the Holy Spirit produces this kind of fruit in our lives; love, joy, peace, patience, kindness, goodness, faithfulness, gentleness, and self-control. Galatians 5:22-23

Bearing these fruits is possible for one reason – Jesus lives in you and if you allow Him, He will live through you.

My old self has been crucified with Christ. It is no longer I who live, but Christ lives in me. So I live in this earthly body by trusting in the Son of God, who loved me and gave himself for me.
Galatians 2:20

Put on all of God's armor so that you will be able to stand firm against all strategies of the devil. Ephesians 6:11

When the Holy Spirit nudges us to submit and show respect, it can take every ounce of energy to push aside our fleshly instincts and obey. That's when we go to the Father for help. There is where we find our strength – when we ask God to give us a spirit of obedience, words of patience, eyes of kindness, and acts of love.

When you say yes to the Holy Spirit's nudging, I can tell you from experience you will not be searching for the right words to speak. They may even sound crazy in your head. It will take the spiritual equivalent of doing a physical chin up to actually utter them.

No temptation has over taken you that is not common to man. God is faithful, and he will not let you be tempted beyond your ability, but with the temptation he will also provide the way of escape, that you may be able to endure it. 1 Corinthians 10:13

I remember a time when all I wanted to do was berate my husband for what I felt had been an injustice to me. I was hurting. I had an arsenal of words at the ready, each perfectly orchestrated to tear him down and make him hurt right along with me. The Holy Spirit said no.

Tell him you love him.

I grit my teeth in silence. Absolutely not. Not right now. That doesn't even make sense.

Tell him you love him. Just say, I love you.

I don't FEEL love right now.

And you won't, not until you make the decision to.

Silence.

Amy, the moment's ending. Your opportunity to obey is fading. You must tell him now.

Deep breath...

I love you.

I said it so softly, he didn't understand. *What did you say?*

Clearing my throat...I love you.

I wasn't smiling when I said it. I wasn't even directly looking at him. Inside, I could feel the battle waging between flesh and spirit. But I was confident, the spirit was speaking truth and my flesh was lying to me. In that moment of obedience, my heart softened. Remember, God will not ignore your effort. Just obey.

Did my husband and I later talk about what upset me? Yes. Was it a different conversation because I obeyed God earlier and told my husband I loved him? Definitely. We were closer, having a better understanding of one another after. I actually felt more love for him than before the hurt. Obedience is difficult. It can also be rewarding.

In the same way, you wives must accept the authority of your husbands. Then even if some refuse to obey the Good News, your godly lives will speak to them without any words. They will be won over by observing your pure and reverent lives. 1 Peter 3:1-2

There's no getting around it. All of this is far easier when you and your husband are in spiritual agreement. It has to be more than a head knowledge that God is in charge. It has to be a heart belief, a full surrender to God's unchanging ways rather than your swaying emotions.

The bible clearly lines out God's plan for marriage, and ideally both spouses realize they answer to Him as well as each other. When only one embraces God's instruction, it's like trying to play football against a team who has completely abandoned the rulebook.

I've seen friends in this exact situation. It's difficult. Frustrating. But not impossible. If you're in a marriage where your husband isn't a Christian, or isn't fulfilling the role God called him to, remain faithful in your obedience.

Your actions will not only strengthen your relationship with the Lord; your husband will be unable to ignore it.

Why? Because few things hit you square in the heart like witnessing someone act out of love without expecting anything in return. When you put your husband's needs before your own – knowing full well he may or may not reciprocate – that's a picture of Jesus. He sacrificed himself for all. He blesses us, courts us, loves us – knowing there is a chance some will never return His love.

Chapter 10
WHILE

But God showed his great love for us by sending Christ to die for us while we were still sinners. Romans 5:8

We will never fix our husband's faults by fixating on them. Deep down, we know this. Yet we devote hours of mental energy to dissecting what we perceive to be their shortcomings. And if we're honest, it all comes back to us fighting for what we think we deserve. Praise God He doesn't give us what we deserve.

Because of our sin, we deserve death and an eternity spent away from His presence. Yet while we were still sinners, He showed us mercy. If He'd waited until we cleaned up our act, we would've never tasted salvation. We'd still be lost as the day is long. He showed us unconditional love while we were utterly disappointing. While we were completely unclean.

So don't wait for your husband to measure up. Love him *while* not *after.*

It's far more productive than digging your heels in with mandates. *"I'll do right by him when he (fill in the blank)."*

Eventually you become someone even you wouldn't want to be around. Bitter. Discontent. Cynical. That good-hearted woman is slowly buried beneath an angry, crusty, heartsick human you never wanted to become.

So pull your heels out of the mud and start acting upon things you can control – your own behavior. You can honor your husband and God by choosing love.

Marriage isn't a staring contest. Don't let days or months go by, hoping he'll blink first and start fulfilling all your needs. The sooner you humble yourself – mimicking your Savior – and begin loving your husband in a selfless way, the sooner you'll see the fruits.

Therefore, confess your sins to one another and pray for one another, that you may be healed. The prayer of a righteous person has great power as it is working. James 5:16

Here's something that will change your marriage practically overnight. Pray for your husband first. Before you present your needs to God, commit to spending time praying for your husband's health, his job and his witness. Pray for his relationship with God to flourish. If he doesn't have a relationship with God, pray for his salvation.

Pray for his connection with his children. Ask God to remove temptation from his path. Pray that your husband finds you beautiful and desirable. Be prepared for these prayers to work – I've experienced it firsthand and it is powerful.

And this is the confidence that we have toward him, that if we ask anything according to his will he hears us. And if we know that he hears us in whatever we ask, we know that we have the requests that we have asked of him. 1 John 5:14-15

Set a guard over my mouth, Lord; keep watch over the door of my lips. Psalm 141:3

One of our constant prayers should be that we're a blessing to our husband. And because we know our spouse best, we know what blesses him most. It usually doesn't have to be a grand gesture. For instance, I've learned my husband really appreciates it when I make a pitcher of tea for him. Sounds random, I know. I do many more time intensive things for him and our family on any given day. So what's the big deal about tea? Eventually I realized all I need to know is it's a blessing to him.

Of course the flip side of being a blessing is being a burden. And no one wants to be thought of that way. I remember years before I got married, a friend gave me a valuable piece of advice:

Don't dump complaints on your husband in the first 30 minutes after he gets home.

What a nugget of wisdom. I never want my husband to hesitate unlocking the front door out of fear or dread of what awaits him inside. I want him to look forward to my smile and kiss. So I hold off on the *"You need to fix the toilet, my boss totally raked me over the coals today, you won't believe how crazy our child is acting."*

I never know what kind of day he's just left behind at the office. Maybe he needs me to listen. Maybe he needs quiet. Maybe he needs a hug or a quick story about something funny our son did that day. So I try to read him rather than greeting him with demands. If you happen to get home at the same time or after your husband, you can still protect that first half hour of interaction. It's worth it. When we give our husbands time to decompress, it's likely they'll be in a better frame of mind to earnestly listen and help us.

It really comes back to the golden rule, also known as Luke 6:31. *"Do unto others as you would have them do unto you."*

Chapter 11
A CHERISHED INHERITANCE

A healthy marriage is a priceless example for your children. For daughters, you're presenting the balanced relationship God intended instead of an unceasing power struggle. As you respect and submit to your husband, you give him a wide open door thru which he can walk in and love you fully, just as Christ loves the church. Selflessly, unabashedly, even to the point of death.

Because of this, your daughters are more likely to hold boyfriends and potential husbands to a higher standard. She will know what it looks like to be valued and adored. She'll understand how to respond in the mountains and valleys. She'll be less likely to settle for a marriage based on fleeting passion or ungodly character. She will have your obedient, beautiful strength to mimic. She will see the importance of choosing a man with the character and faith to appreciate, embrace, and honor her.

Your sons will be more inclined to seek a woman with a heart for God, one who can respect him and love him as God intended. He will grow up observing your grace and carefully chosen speech.

When she speaks, her words are wise, and she gives instructions with kindness. Proverbs 31:26

Your sons will see the fruits of a marriage where God is first. Where momma is wise and treasured. Where daddy is respected, responsible and strong. He will see how consistently sewing seeds of love in a wife's heart will bless him and his entire family.

This is when we see the fruit of our obedience multiplying through generations. And while there is no guarantee our children will follow in our footsteps, we must – with prayer and confidence – give them the most blessed footsteps to follow.

Chapter 12
EXPECTATIONS

When you decide to trust God's ways for marriage above your own, get ready. Things will change. And how could they not? The essence of biblical submission and respect goes against everything the world preaches and practices. You're no longer determining how you treat your husband based on his behavior. You're loving selflessly and fully like Jesus.

There will be days where the fruits of your obedience wash over old scars in your marriage like a soothing balm. For the newlywed, you'll notice your relationship involves much less drama than other couples'. It really should be no surprise that respect, love and the absence of a power struggle produces harmony. But it takes faith to put that formula in motion.

And know from the beginning, you will mess up. Sometimes the days will be long and your patience will run short. Your flesh will fail you and your tongue will get ahead of your heart. You'll say and do things you wish you hadn't. So you ask for forgiveness, which God has promised and Jesus secured. You apologize to your husband. And you forgive yourself. Because this isn't about being perfect, it's about obedience, grace and love.

The enemy will tell you it's just too hard, that you may as well give up. Why? Because a strong Christian marriage is a great threat to his mission. A strong Christian marriage is a light to the world. It's a witness to your children. It brings glory to God. So recognize the enemy's lies for what they are – an attack on your marriage and life.

Submit yourselves, then, to God. Resist the devil, and he will flee from you. James 4:7

Here's a hard truth. While following God's command to let your husband lead increases your odds for a healthy marriage, it doesn't ensure a perfect marriage. It doesn't even guarantee a good one.

Not what you wanted to hear, I know.

Because God gives people free will, there are a multitude of factors out of our control. Maybe your spouse refuses to move beyond the damage that's already been done. Maybe he's making lifestyle choices that make a healthy marriage all but impossible. Things like drug use, an extramarital affair, physical or emotional abuse. In an abusive marriage, the first concern is for your safety. Remove yourself from danger, get to a safe place, seek Christian counsel and pray about next steps.

So, if success isn't guaranteed, how can I be so passionate about biblical submission? For starters, of the marriages I've known where God's design isn't embraced, the vast majority failed painfully for both parties. Those where God's instruction is respected and followed – for the most part – flourish. They are markedly different.

Closer to home, after witnessing the destructive pattern of divorce in my family, I threw off the lies the world had sold me. I trusted God's truth. Every day since, I've watched the blessings unfold. Every day. Even the tough ones are better because of the relationship He's given me. His way has not only made my marriage better, stronger, and more joyful; it's downright fun.

But this really comes back to my relationship with God. I choose His ways because I love Him, and obedience is how I show it.

Those who accept my commandments and obey them are the ones who love me. And because they love me, my Father will love them. And I will love them and reveal myself to each of them. John 14:21

So will your marriage become harmonious, enjoyable, passionate – all the things you're hoping? You certainly have a better shot if you embrace God's ways than if you ignore His commands. Regardless of your husband's choices or responses to your Godly obedience, you are walking in God's will. There's no better, safer place to be.

It may sound contradictory, but submission takes strength. And the more you do it, the stronger you get. Here is the stand-up-and-shout good news – it also gets easier. In my experience, just as our body has muscle memory, our spirit has behavioral memory. Being obedient, respectful, and submissive does more than become second nature – it actually *becomes your nature*.

You'll notice the internal struggle is no longer nearly as intense. The devil is losing his influence on your life. Deeply rooted patterns of stubbornness, selfishness and bitterness have been replaced with fresh soil useful to God Almighty. Your habit of choosing the right words, the right countenance, is becoming beautifully predictable. You are looking in the mirror and seeing the wife God created you to be. Your husband will without doubt see her too. His response – whether it comes instantly or over years – can make your heart swell with gratitude.

And should you doubt, thinking it was easier for me to submit than it might be for you, just listen to the lies the world would have me believe. Because I am ten years older than my husband, I must be wiser than he. Because I have a college degree and my husband does not, I must be more valuable. Because I've lived in many places and had more life experiences, I am better equipped to lead. Those are only true in the world's economy.

Here is the eternal truth God has used to set me free. My age, my education, my experiences are all part of me. But they in no way alter His design for marriage. Because His commands are perfect, they hold true for every marriage.

Yes, my husband finds my intelligence sexy. He finds my experiences interesting. But above and far beyond all of that, he finds my submissive heart so beautiful he can't resist loving me as Christ loves the church.

Her husband praises her: "There are many virtuous and capable women in the world, but you surpass them all!" Proverbs 31:28-29

My husband loves me more deeply, sweetly, and passionately than I imagined possible. God blesses my obedience. God blesses our marriage. God gives me strength and immeasurable joy through submission.

And that, my friends...is why I am smiling.

* * * *

SALVATION

In His abundant mercy and love, God has made a way for us to become His children. Some would say that because God made us, we are born His children. But that was a physical birth. You must have a spirit birth to be transformed from this life, to everlasting life with Him.

I've heard many say, "*I believe in God.*" The danger there is that merely believing in God is not the same as putting your full trust in Him to save you.

You say you have faith, for you believe that there is one God. Good for you! Even the demons believe this, and they tremble in terror. James 2:19

At this point, you may be thinking that your life doesn't reflect God, that you aren't worthy of salvation. No human can ever clean themselves up enough to be worthy. God saves us purely through the worthiness of Jesus. He was the perfect sacrifice, something we could never be, paying a price higher than we could ever pay.

With Jesus' last breath on the cross he said, "*It is finished.*"

Everything that needed to be done to save us had been completed. He kept His promise by rising from the dead three days later, and has been inviting sinners to put their faith in Him ever since.

Behold, I stand at the door and knock. If anyone hears my voice and opens the door, I will come in to him. Revelation 3:20a

If your heart is telling you now is the time, these life-changing verses will walk you through the decision.

For everyone has sinned; we all fall short of God's glorious standard. Romans 3:23

For the wages of sin is death, but the free gift of God is eternal life through Christ Jesus our Lord. Romans 6:23

Worse than a physical death, spiritual death sends us to a literal hell and separates us from God for all eternity. But praise God, salvation is a free gift. You cannot earn it, you must simply receive it.

But God showed his great love for us by sending Christ to die for us while we were still sinners. Romans 5:8

His love saves us; not religion or church membership.

Everyone who calls on the name of the Lord will be saved. Romans 10:13

If you confess with your mouth that Jesus is Lord and believe in your heart that God raised him from the dead, you will be saved. For it is believing in your heart that you are made right with God, and it is confessing with your mouth that you are saved. Romans 10:9-10

You can pray this right now, right where you are.

"Dear God, I confess that I am a sinner, and I am sorry. I need a Savior. I believe that Jesus, your Son, died on the cross to be my Savior. I believe He arose from the grave to live as my Lord. I turn from my sin. I ask You, Lord Jesus to forgive my sin and come into my heart. I trust you as my Savior and receive you as my Lord. Thank you, Jesus, for saving me."

If you genuinely prayed that prayer of repentance and faith, you are saved. You have God's word on it. I encourage you to record this moment inside your bible to serve as a beautiful reminder.

I, (insert name), on (insert date), repent of my sin and accept Jesus Christ as my personal Lord and Savior. According to the promise of God in Romans 10:13, I have called upon His name and have His word for the assurance of my salvation.

Congratulations! The angels of heaven rejoice with you. Without question, it is the wisest decision you will ever make.

Likewise I say unto you, there is joy in the presence of the angels of God over one sinner that repents. Luke 5:10

STUDY GUIDE

Chapter 1: I Get It

1. Before beginning this book, what was your view of submission?

2. Jot down any aspects of submission that make you nervous or fearful.

3. How can God help you with those feelings?

Read 2 Timothy 1:7 and Psalm 28:6-7

4. What about submission gives you hope for your marriage?

5. Ask God to prepare your heart to fully embrace his commands. Talk with him about your fears and hopes.

Chapter 2: The First Test

1. What has God asked of you in your marriage that you're hesitating or refusing to do?

2. When thinking about God's design for marriage, what outcome are you imagining that makes you skeptical, nervous or rebellious?

3. What good could come from your obedience in this area?

4. Write down the steps or actions of obedience you are willing to take.

Read Proverbs 3:3-8

Chapter 3: The Heart

1. Write this C.S. Lewis quote on something and place it where you'll see it daily.

"True humility is not thinking less of yourself, it's thinking of yourself less."

2. Think of a person you know who is humble. Jot down something they have said or done to show humility.

3. When you think about what this person did – or how they live their life – does it cause you to see them as weak?

Read Colossians 3:12

4. Write down instances where you tend to be stubborn or prideful.

5. Take a few moments to pray and ask God to help you see the beauty and necessity of humility.

Chapter 4: Dropping the "If"

1. Do you think your husband deserves your respect or submission? Why or why not? (And don't just give the answer you think is correct; be really honest. God already knows what you're thinking.)

2. If you choose to disobey the command to respect your husband and submit to him, what message does that send God?

Read Matthew 6:14-15

3. Lay your husband's offenses at the foot of the cross. They are no longer yours to carry or use as excuses or weapons. Spend a few minutes talking with God about any negative feelings you have toward your spouse. He's your father and loves hearing your honest thoughts. Ask God to heal your mind and heart and to help you release the bitterness that has taken root. Embrace the clean slate that true forgiveness offers.

Chapter 5: Seeds or Weeds

1. What are some things you've said once or multiple times that you know hurt your husband?

2. Now slash through each statement above. Cross them out one by one. Make a conscious decision to remove those statements from your arsenal. In fact, burn your arsenal to the ground. We are not supposed to be at war with the one we pledged to love.

3. Beyond words, in what ways do you punish your husband? Really think here. We women are crafty creatures, so just fess up to some of your best work. And don't forget the little tactics that creep into our daily lives and become habits. (Example: scheduling him for a duty or engagement when you know he has something fun planned with his buddy, simply because you think he's had more than enough "me" time. I just pulled that one out of thin air, of course.)

4. Take a few minutes to ask God for forgiveness. Pray for wisdom in dealing with hurts and frustrations within your marriage.

5. Write down at least 5 of your husband's qualities you most treasure.

6. Make a point to praise him in these areas. And when the opportunity presents itself, talk about his good qualities in front of friends and family. If he happens to hear you, that's certainly not a bad thing.

Chapter 6: Giving it to God

1. In your marriage, what have you been fighting for control of or trying to handle on your own?

2. Write down your prayer concerning this issue. Anytime you feel overwhelmed or that you want to handle it your own way, read your prayer out loud.

Chapter 7: Search My Heart

1. If someone were to ask your husband the main things you bug (nag) him about, what would he say?

2. Take a few moments to pray about each of these things. If you're feeling bold, sit your husband down and tell him you are trusting God with these things and that you aren't going to hound him anymore. Scary stuff, right? Just remember, you are not alone in this.

Read Deuteronomy 31:8

Chapter 8: The Helper

1. In which areas can you be more of a willing helper to your husband?

2. Jot down gifts he's given your husband that you do not have. Now, write down gifts God has given you that your husband does not have.

3. How can you use your gifts (joyfully not begrudgingly) to bless your spouse and family?

4. Which areas of your marriage create the most friction? How could your being respectful and submissive alleviate some of the struggle?

5. Consider telling your husband that he can expect your support going forward. Let him know you're trusting him and God for the best outcome in these areas.

6. Feeling extra daring? Fully embrace the role of a servant like Jesus did during his earthly ministry. Set aside time one evening to wash your husband's feet. I'm serious. Make it a special, quiet experience. You both will likely be uncomfortable at first. But in my experience this act of love connects you on a deeper level than either of you might imagine.

Chapter 9: Tossing the Scorecard

1. Make a conscious decision to release your husband from his debts to you. These debts could be hurts, disappointments, or areas where you feel as though you always "out do" him. Instead of viewing your efforts and actions as "credits" you stack on your side of the scale, see them purely as gifts to your spouse that require no payback. Talk with God about this for a few minutes.

2. Who is the most selfless, generous person in your marriage? (Hint: you should aim for it to be you.) Write down ways in which you can surprise and bless your spouse through selfless, giving gestures. They don't have to be grand gestures. Think everyday opportunities here.

Read: Psalm 37:3-9

3. Pray and ask God to help you be more aware of and sensitive to the Holy Spirit's promptings.

4. Write down common results of people being stubborn.

5. Write down common results of people being selfless.

Read 1 Corinthians 13:1-3

6. If your husband is not a Christian, write down the names of some trusted friends and fellow believers you can ask to join you in prayer for his salvation.

Chapter 10: While

1. What does your husband do that most frustrates/hurts/drives you crazy?

2. If he never stops doing it, can you still respect him and submit to him? Will you? Talk with God about it now.

3. What could you be praying about for your husband? Be specific. Think about his health, his job, relationships, witness, etc. Write them down and be persistent in your praying.

Read Luke 18:1-8

Chapter 11: A Cherished Inheritance

1. If you have children, think back to times they've witnessed you disrespect your husband. Maybe there are two instances. Maybe there are countless. Decide now that going forward, they will see your respect for their father and your love for your heavenly Father. If they're old enough to notice the change and ask you about it, be honest and open. This can be an incredible witness and teaching moment with your children.

2. If you don't have children, think of people in your circle of influence who would benefit from seeing your marriage transform and blossom. Their questions may bring about an opportunity to share your testimony. Remember, this is bigger than marriage. This is about glorifying God.

3. Talk to God about using your marriage as a shining light in this world of cynics. Be bold in your prayer.

Read Hebrews 4:16 and Ephesians 3:20-21

Chapter 12: Expectations

1. What blessings do you expect or hope for in your marriage?

2. How do you anticipate obedience will affect your relationship with God?

3. If the only blessing is a stronger, better, closer relationship with God – is it worth it? Would that be enough?

Read Philippians 4:12-13

4. Think of a Christian friend, family member or mentor with whom you can confide in throughout this journey. Choose someone who will encourage you and pray for your family. Reach out to them; let them know about your plans to follow God's commands for marriage.

5. Journal your struggles, victories and prayers during this new chapter in your marriage. You never know when you'll need to look back for encouragement or use your experience to encourage someone else.

Read Romans 8:37-39

I'm so excited you're choosing to run toward God's freedom and the blessings He has for you. I'm praying for restored, thriving marriages throughout the world. Feel free to connect with me via Facebook or email.

ABOUT THE AUTHOR

Amy Williams is a happy mama, grateful Christian, and wife who still has a major crush on her husband. She writes from her home in a one-stoplight Oklahoma town, taking breaks to pray, make more coffee, and bust a move. Living room dancing is crucial to her writing process.

She's a proud alumna of Oklahoma State University, and has lived in six different states throughout the South and Midwest. Amy is passionate about helping people experience vibrant marriages. The kind where you truly look forward to seeing your spouse at the end of each day.

Connect with her at:
www.facebook.com/amyhopkinswilliamsauthor
amywilliamsauthor@yahoo.com

Made in the USA
Lexington, KY
30 October 2016